A
O.

"Veteran, versatile singer/songwriter Aaron Espe's new book is a remarkable and inspiring and courageous feat. It is a methodical and engaging deep-dive into the songwriting process, exploring creative psychology and providing useful tips to stay fresh through the ebbs and flows of songwriter life and craft. Above all, this book will challenge your thinking and, dare I say, perhaps make you a better writer after all is said and done. This meat and potatoes songwriting manual is a welcomed addition to the genre and has the makings of essential reading."

—DOUG WATERMAN, former Editor in Chief of *AMERICAN SONGWRITER*

"Aaron cuts through the noise and the lingo to offer the cleanest line, the least distracting path to answering the question of "what do I do next?" The confidence that comes from reading Aaron's holistic and digestible way of viewing the job, the industry and the human spirit of writing, will lead folks to learn more, try more and succeed sooner. It is the perfect launchpad for any aspiring songwriter."

—BARRY DEAN, Grammy-nominated hit songwriter (Little Big Town, Tenille Townes, Ingrid Michaelson)

"With Espe's trademark gentle humor and razor wit, he creaks opens the ominous door marked 'Pro Songwriting' and casually flicks the light on. This is an invaluable read for anyone ready to finally get those songs out that have been rattling around in their soul and maybe even quit their job while they're at it."

—ISAAC SLADE, co-founder of Grammy-nominated band, The Fray

"I wish Espe had written this 20 years ago and I had stumbled across it in a Border's."

—BEN WEST, hit songwriter and producer (P!nk, Tim McGraw, Lady Antebellum)

"After reading this book I've realized Aaron Espe is not only a very talented songwriter but gifted at teaching and explaining how something works so that anyone can understand it. That's not an easy thing to do. I honestly haven't thought of songwriting in some of the ways he explains in this book and I think that's the beauty of learning from one another. Aaron has a quiet, gentle soul and that's just one of the reasons I love him and his songwriting. He really tries to nail a story within a song and he usually succeeds."

—PHILLIP PHILLIPS, certified Platinum recording artist, songwriter, and 2012 *American Idol* winner

"…This is so helpful, accurate, and needed."

—LEIGH NASH, lead vocalist of Grammy-nominated band, Sixpence None the Richer

"It is vital for books about songwriting to be written by someone who is actually a songwriter and who has songs that are out in the world. I have now taught at Belmont, at MTSU, and private workshops. Sometimes people who are great at marketing themselves are not actually songwriters. That is part of why I feel [Espe's] book is important. People can learn from someone who has actually sat in a studio / a room and written a song."

—BONNIE BAKER, hit songwriter (Reba McEntire, Hunter Hayes, Rachel Platten) and adjunct professor, MTSU

"This book is overflowing with insightful, practical, big-hearted advice for every songwriter who aspires to write truer, richer, and more memorable songs. Aaron drops so much humor and wisdom in this book that you will need a baseball glove if you want to catch it all. Whether you've been playing music for two days or twenty years, this book will inspire, encourage, and liberate the songwriter within you."

—GRETA MORGAN, singer-songwriter and multi-instrumentalist (The Hush Sound, Springtime Carnivore, Vampire Weekend)

ON SONG-WRITING

PRACTICAL TIPS AND INSIGHTS
FROM A DECADE IN MUSIC CITY

AARON ESPE

Copyright © 2023 Aaron Espe

All rights reserved. No portion of this book may be reproduced, stored in a retrieval system, or transmitted in any form or by any means—electronic, mechanical, photocopy, recording, scanning, or other—except for brief quotations in critical reviews or articles, without the prior written permission of the publisher.

ISBN: 979-8-8602-5840-2

In memory of Busbee (1976–2019), my friend and mentor of thirteen years. He taught me about songwriting, but mostly about how to share your life and help others. You are missed.

CONTENTS

FOREWARD   i
INTRODUCTION   iii

ON CRAFT

Only Two Ways to Write a Song	7
Writing Melodies	9
Showing vs. Telling	11
Idea Over Rhyme	12
Sprinkling Contrast	14
Nursery Rhymes	15
Coming Up with Unique Metaphors	16
Word Pools	18
Switching Up Mediums	19
The Dad-Joke Filter	21
Check Your Verb-Tense	23
It's Usually the Simplest Way	24
What's Your Antithesis?	25
3 Questions to Break the Curse of Knowledge	26
Rewrite It	28

ON MINDSET

Happy Accidents (or Action-Dents)	32
If You Lack Life Experience	34
Let People Put You In a Box	35
It's Like Naming a Child	36

Discovering Your Unique Voice	37
Is This Song Any Good?	38
What's the Bigger Truth?	39
Be Unoriginal	41
Boring Life Is Interesting	43
Fairy Dust and Work Ethic	44
Write What You Don't Know	45
Make It Easy	46
Update Your Brain's Operating System	47
Paint with the Brushes You Have	48
Two Is One	49
The Calendar Hack	50

ON DEALING WITH YOUR INNER CRITIC

Before Anyone Hurts Your Feelings	54
5-4-3-2-1	55
Use Your Jealousy for Good	56
Nervous Is Normal	57
Shushing	58
Doubting the Vision	59
Disappointment Is Your Friend	60
Be a Character We'd Love In a Movie	61
Imposter Syndrome	63

ON COWRITING

What's Cowriting?	66

Avoiding the Awkward Start	67
Commitment Issues	68
Wanted: Dumb Ideas	69
How to Be My Substitute Cowriter	70

ON MUSIC CITY AND THE INDUSTRY

Should You Move to Nashville?	76
Hang with Your High School Classmates	77
Choosing Your Path	78
See Yourself As a Small Business	79
What's Your 80/20?	81
The Pub and the Master	83
Curiosity and Conscience	85
Go Easy on the Victim Songs	87
Could Mister Rogers Sing This?	89
The "Will I Be Successful" Test	90
Cross Your Fingers, but Don't Hold Your Breath	91
Sustaining a Career	92

EPILOGUE

    Lessons From a Hit Songwriter's Funeral   93

APPENDIX: CHEAT SHEETS

    How to Get Unstuck   97

    Instead of Theory Learn This   99

    How to Structure a Basic Song   101

    Do Your Song This Meta Favor   104

    Rules for TV Ads   109

    Five Strangely Effective Prompts   111

ACKNOWLEDGEMENTS   113
ABOUT THE AUTHOR   115

FOREWARD

I first met Aaron Espe when he was the frontman for Bombs Over Nowhere. In the decade since, I've come to know him as a friend, a co-writer and a phenomenal talent. The bio will tell you about his career achievements and the front flap will generally describe the contents of the book, so what is left for this foreword? My answer is simple: a frame to see the picture through. A way to understand how this new book can serve, inspire and inform your journey.

Aaron Espe is a recording artist, songwriter and producer with his work on records, commercials, tv and film, but he is also an incredible painter. His beautiful watercolors provide a visual analogy for the way he writes and produces. He captures the essence of a place, the power of an experience, the truth of a feeling. He never belabors, cheapens or hides it. Every piece provides you the things you need and nothing to distract you from the moment he is capturing. You can see that singular approach in his visual art, hear it in the creativity of music, and feel it when you read this book.

I've spent almost twenty years in Nashville as a songwriter and occasional producer. I've been fortunate to have hits and, just as fortunate, to survive the droughts between them. All the while, I've read any books or articles on the process, craft and life of songwriting I could get my hands on. Aaron's new book provides the fastest, most effective place to start for a new writer. Every new writer I know has lots of questions, just like I did, on a variety of topics from inspiration to how the business works. *On Songwriting* cuts through the noise and the lingo to offer the cleanest line, the least distracting path to answering the question of "what do I do next?" The confidence that comes from reading Aaron's holistic and digestible way of viewing the job, the industry and the human spirit of writing, will lead folks to learn more, try more and succeed sooner. It is the perfect launchpad for any aspiring songwriter.

Aaron has juggled the many roles that the modern business demands and has shaped a book for the new industry, where one person must wear many hats. Songwriter, producer, publisher, and even a self-guided record label—he has provided enough to bring clarity and understanding without diving too deep or obscuring the way forward with too much detail on the map. He has done in this book what he does in his songs and his watercolors—giving you the platform and tools you need to start your own story.

There is, however, another way the book delighted me. I found myself using it like a creative devotional. Reading a chapter or two every morning along with my other rituals. I had expected to find a book for beginners but found it to be a daily encouragement and a lens to focus my view of the work at hand.

I would be remiss if I didn't mention the appendixes. Do not sleep on this section of the book. There is much value in those few pages which are easily ignored in most books.

Whenever we are starting out in something, anything from first love to new job to writing songs, we can be quickly overwhelmed by how little experience we have. But, I think the less talked about part that we almost drown in, is how much there is to know. I would argue it is the size of the unknown ocean that makes us shrink away from it, at first. Sometimes, just in time, a friend, a colleague, or a teacher helps us start. They help us see that we can understand and succeed, and in those first successes we find our first "lucky break" toward achieving our dreams. I think this little book will be like that for lots of people.

All the best,

—Barry Dean

INTRODUCTION

I wrote this little book for six people.

The first is a singer-songwriter I once knew. It was 2011 and he and his wife packed up all their belongings (mostly guitars) and drove across the country to start fresh in Nashville, Tennessee. They had no money. This singer-songwriter had his sights set on a publishing deal, even though he didn't know what a publishing deal was exactly. He'd never cowritten. Never had a licensing placement. He didn't know his songs weren't very good. That no other artist would want to record them until he wrote better ones.

So what did he have?

An insatiable desire to learn, and the drive to put it into practice. Maybe you've guessed. This first person was me over ten years ago.

The second person (and third, fourth, and fifth) I wrote this little book for are my sons. The eldest just turned ten. I don't know if any of them will want to follow in their father's footsteps. Part of me, admittedly most of me, hopes they do not. It's a difficult path with no guarantees. But if any one of them does, then I would share with them everything I've learned about songwriting and the pursuit of it as a vocation. I would write it out as clearly as possible and explain—short, sweet, and hopefully a little entertaining—the most helpful lessons I've learned in the last ten years.

The sixth and last person I wrote this for is you. It's likely you've got songs inside you that you think are worth chasing. You want to learn and grow, take your art more seriously, maybe even pursue it as a career. Then at the very least I hope you find this book helpful. At most, I hope it inspires you to keep going, to keep striving to be better and get more of your art into the world for others to experience. I'll be right there with you trying to do the same. Best of luck!

—Aaron

ON CRAFT

"You just have to be smarter than the wood."
—My old construction boss

— On Craft —

ONLY TWO WAYS TO WRITE A SONG

There are only two ways to write a song. Okay, sure, there are plenty more. But what I've found is it primarily comes down to these two: you can paint or you can use the GPS method.

1. The GPS Method

I'm calling it the GPS method because when you're approaching songwriting this way, you know the destination, you just don't know how to get there. It's like a friend sending you the address to a new restaurant. You punch it into Maps, Google Maps, or perhaps by the time you're reading this it's some other newfangled technology, and you let the GPS reverse engineer the path from where you want to be to where you currently are.

In this case, the hook—the memorable part of the song—is the address. And usually the hook is what you have first. The hook could be a title you've been wanting to use, or a phrase you overheard someone say. It could also be a melodic shape or a guitar riff. Whatever the hook is, you know it's your destination, it's the the thing that's most important. So you reverse engineer the song to that. Let me give you a personal example.

I had the title "Things I've Never Seen" in my Notes app. I didn't have a melody. I didn't have any chords or melodic shapes. Just a title, an "address." I knew the song would be about—yes, things I've never seen—but I didn't know if it was a serious or reflective song. Was it about cities I've never been to or landmarks? I didn't know. I eventually chose to make it a silly type of children's song about things I've never seen; a list of items that ended at my title (destination).

> *A cow running in the pasture*
> *My mailman in regular clothes*
> *A secret getting past my mother*
> *My father touching his toes*
>
> *They're more alike than different*
> *At least they are to me*
> *These are just a few*
> *Things I've never seen*

2. The Painting Method

Painting is far different from the GPS method because you're not starting with a hook. You don't have a title or any concrete lyrics. You don't have a clear concept of where you're going or what your destination is.

What you do have is a mood, a sense of what the song should feel like. I call this the painting method because it's a more elusive process. It reminds me of an abstract painter standing in front of a blank canvas, beginning with a brush stroke here, a brush stroke there.

The painting method isn't as much about the song as the process of writing the song. It's an experience. Anything could happen. You unfold the song rather than reverse engineer it.

One song I wrote recently using this method is called "Isn't It Good." When I started, I didn't have any lyrics or melodic shapes. I simply was in a mood, wanting to slow down in life and be more present. I sat on the couch, stared out the window, and started finger picking some chords while humming little bits of gibberish over it. A few hours later the song was finished.

Side note: The two methods can overlap. Sometimes you'll be using the GPS method and thinking you know the destination. But then you realize you're going somewhere else. Be open to it. Or sometimes you'll be painting but realize you have a lot of ideas formed that could benefit from a more structured, reverse-engineered approach. Be open to that as well. A good rule of thumb is to always keep an open mind. Songwriting, no matter what method you use, is still incredibly mysterious. Whenever you finish a song you'll find yourself thinking, "Well, I have no idea how that happened!"

— On Craft —

WRITING MELODIES

I have this recurring dream. I'm on stage performing in front of a crowd, but I forget the words and melody. I start making up gibberish. Gibberish words over gibberish melodies while I strum my guitar. It's like I'm scatting, but it's not supposed to sound improvised. It's supposed to sound like completed lyrics and melodies. Good ones, too. The kind people pay money to come and listen to. My goal in the dream is to get close enough to actual sounding lyrics so I can blame the sound person for any listener complaints. I do this for a fairly long time until I wake up.

I've talked to enough songwriters who have the same recurring dream to know it's a "thing." Maybe you've experienced it, too. I bring it up because my approach to writing melodies in the dream is pretty similar to my approach in real life (minus the cold sweats). It's making stuff up in the moment, seeing what feels good. You're kind of just scatting with words, vowel sounds, melodic shapes until the pieces start to fit like a puzzle.

Imagine someone said, "Start whistling a made up tune right now." Do you know what you'd do? You'd start by whistling one note until you moved onto another and another.

I'll be honest, writing melody is difficult to describe because, for me, it's mostly intuition. I don't write anything down. I don't know what notes I'm singing. I improvise until eventually I keep singing the same thing in the same places.

If I'm writing with other people, one of us is improvising while the other is listening and writing. "Oh, I love that melody," I'll say, then sing it back to them. We might record that clip so we don't forget it. This goes on and on until we have all our melodic "shapes." One shape for the verses, one for the chorus, one for the bridge, and maybe some ad lib stuff, here and there.

But it's all just going for it and having fun. Not worrying whether you're copying somebody else or whether anybody's watching. You're just trying to feel it out until your melodies are complimenting your lyrics and vice versa.

This little book won't dive very deep into melody, because for me and most writers I know it's an intuitive process. However, if you want to geek out on writing melodies, I highly recommend the book *Tunesmith* by Jimmy Webb. He goes into more technical depth on the subject.

— On Craft —

SHOWING VS. TELLING

You probably remember your high school English teacher talking about how you should show more than you tell. Still, let's cover it here. It's easy to gloss over and think you're doing it. But if you really comb through your song and try to hear it from the listener's perspective, you'll probably find that you're telling too much and not showing enough.

Ok, let's make this a little more concrete.

It's ok to tell a bit. "I love you." That's telling.

"I think about you everyday" is showing.

But you could show more. "I daydream about your smile." That's more. Or even more: "The car behind me honked me out of a daydream about your smile."

Do you see what I'm getting at?

Think of telling as a claim. Think of showing as evidence you need to backup your claim.

If you're going to do more telling, do that in the chorus. Choruses—especially in popular music—are a great place to tell more than show. You don't want to bog your listener down with too much information in the chorus. Keep it simple and singable.

But in your verses, you have more freedom to show. Use imagery, get descriptive. Take the listener into your world and let them get lost in the moment.

— On Craft —

IDEA OVER RHYME

It's easy as a songwriter to get overly concerned about rhyming. Don't get me wrong, I think rhyming is important. But it shouldn't control the song's narrative.

Here's an example of when I let rhyming win instead of the song's theme. The song is about my family's first vacation to Disney World.

Verse one goes like this:

> *When I was nine years old,*
> *My parents told me:*
> *"We're gonna take a vacation.*
> *We're going somewhere,*
> *A place where people only care,*
> *About relaxation.*

"Vacation" and "relaxation" is a nice rhyme, sure, but let's think more about it. Is it intuitive? Does the statement ring completely true? I would argue, not quite. After all, people don't go to Disney World to relax. They go because it's the happiest place on earth. "How was your time at Disney World?" "Oh, it was very relaxing, thank you." Nobody has ever said that. In fact, parents might tell you it's one of the most stressful places on earth!

Instead, I should have used a slant rhyme and paired "vacation" with "happy" or some other word closer to the essence of Disney World. I also could have moved things around so "vacation" didn't land at the end of the line, which would free me up to rhyme different words.

It's not terrible the way it is, but it could be better. My point in all this is to remind you that you have options. Your idea can always beat the rhyme. And when your idea wins, it resonates more with the listener. It's a truer feeling. Plus, don't forget that lyrics have the luxury of being sung. Imperfect rhymes that are sung tend to sound more perfect than they look on the page.

When in doubt, choose the idea over the rhyme.

— On Craft —

SPRINKLING CONTRAST

When I was a kid, I only knew one kind of winter. That was a Minnesota winter. Winter meant cold. It meant icy roads, and walking to school with frost on my eyelashes.

Then one October when I was nine, my family traveled to Florida. We got off the plane and it was hot. I saw a man wearing shorts. I could hardly believe it. Winter in Florida was not winter in Minnesota.

You don't really know what something is until you know what it isn't. This is true in songwriting. If you have a verse that has long notes and a flowing melody, you might want to have a more syncopated chorus with shorter notes. If you have a lot of lyrics in the verses, you might want to have more space in the chorus.

Sprinkle contrast everywhere. It helps listeners appreciate a warm Florida winter because they've experienced the Minnesota cold. If you don't use contrast, your song will feel like one long and boring December.

— On Craft —

NURSERY RHYMES

Sometimes you think you have to reinvent the wheel in your song's rhyming scheme. But often the most basic form will work. It's at least a great starting point.

Think of your favorite nursery rhyme. It will likely be four lines rhyming in aabb.

For example, as you know (or your parents have failed), "Humpty Dumpty" goes like this:

> *Humpty Dumpty sat on a wall*
> *Humpty Dumpty had a great fall*
> *All the king's horses and all the king's men*
> *Couldn't put Humpty together again*

It feels silly and a little dumb, right? But you can use this form loosely with even the most serious subjects. Here, let me make up something rather heartbreaking for the sake of making a point:

> *Maybe it was spring or fall*
> *Truth is, I just can't recall*
> *Much of anything after she passed*
> *Each season's spent wishing her back*

See? Serious topic, silly nursery rhyme form. It works.

Every now and then, try replace your favorite nursery rhyme with original lyrics. It'll help when you're staring at a blank page, and you'll be surprised at how good the form feels.

— On Craft —

COMING UP WITH UNIQUE METAPHORS

Coming up with a great metaphor seems tricky, but it's simpler than you think.

At the end of the day, a great metaphor is you showing the listener how two things they hadn't thought were very similar are actually very much the same. You might think the good ones are already taken, but that's because you're focusing on the ones you know. The ones that haven't been taken are usually the ones right in front of you, in your own life.

The other day I was watching my son and the neighbor kid on the tire swing. I started thinking about old tires and how they've been down so many roads. I let my mind wander on that thought for a while. Then I had this funny idea about two tires on a car having a conversation about the afterlife. It occurred to me that a tire swing is kind of like heaven for a tire. After all the years toiling on hot roads, they finally get to kick their feet up under the shade of a tree in the company of children laughing and singing.

I'm not saying that's the greatest metaphor in the world. But up until that point, I'd never thought of heaven and tire swings as being similar. This is a simple example of paying attention to what's going on around you—keeping your songwriter antenna up for unique metaphors happening in front of you.

You're probably doing something today that you think is mundane. But that's a great litmus test. The stuff that makes you bored is probably because you know it so well. But do others? Think of it from their perspective. Be surprised by the little details. Maybe you're an electrician, and you're very familiar with the attics of people's homes. What's it like up there? Write a song called "Attics" or "Insulation" and tell us how they represent some aspect of everyone's life. Maybe you work the drive-thru window at McDonald's. What do you notice about people? What is it that you're constantly doing that feels similar to something else in life? Are the same people coming through each day? Are there coworkers who get on your nerves? Tell us how a drive-thru is a metaphor for life in some way.

— On Craft —

WORD POOLS

Sometimes I like to write a paragraph or two of what I think my song-in-progress is about. It's not because I think I'll come to any real conclusion. It's because I'm trying to get my brain to give me words around a particular topic.

Once I was trying to write a song about the oil spill in the Gulf of Mexico. But I didn't have enough language surrounding the topic, so I wrote a paragraph. Then I searched Wikipedia and read about the oil spill. I learned words and was reminded of others I'd forgotten. I wrote a few more paragraphs.

Little word pools are helpful because, as you're writing lyrics, you can pull material from them you might not have otherwise come up with.

Bonus tip: Take the paragraph you just wrote, copy and paste it into a program like wordclouds.com or something similar. It will give you a visual of the most repeated nouns, helping you see the idea in a new way. This may help spark a thought or move the song in a different direction.

— On Craft —

SWITCHING UP MEDIUMS

How often do you switch up your medium? Do you always write with pen and paper? iPhone Notes app? Old school typewriter?

This might sound obvious, but writing is all about transferring information—thoughts, ideas, concepts—from your brain to someplace outside of your brain. For doing this, each medium has its benefits and detriments.

For example, if I'm typing on my desktop computer, I'm most comfortable. There's a flow and pattern that's recognizable. My keyboard is familiar. But I also know that I can delete anything. Nothing I write is permanent. So, I'm slightly careless and noncommittal. I type and delete, type and delete. It's easy to start overthinking. Even though the desktop computer is my most comfortable experience, it's often my least productive.

Pen and paper, though? That's a step up. It's more physical work to write something down, assuming you've been typing most of your life. I find when I'm physically writing, my brain commits more to what I'm saying. There's more quality control in its communication to my hand. After all, my brain is aware of the physical stress on my hand. It knows my hand doesn't want to be writing all day.

The manual typewriter is one my favorites. Not just because it looks cool, though it does. But also because it's mechanical and loud and it takes force to stamp the ribbon and transfer ink onto the page. Once the sound picks up and becomes steadier, I feel my brain become almost like a locomotive. Like I'm feeding wood into an old steam engine. If I want to keep the chugging of the typewrite keys going, I need keep typing without overthinking. If I overthink, I'll stop, and it'll take a lot of effort to get back up to speed again. The typewriter is great for unfiltered, "throw up on the page" writing. I use it to get myself out of my head.

If you've been tied to one medium, switch it up. See what happens. Try a range of different methods until you find one that gets your brain working the way you need it to for that particular part of your songwriting process.

— Craft —

THE DAD-JOKE FILTER

If your lyrics lack punch or impact, and it's difficult to know why, try running it through the dad-joke filter. Let me explain. A well-crafted song is like a dad joke. Take this one I heard recently.

Question:
Where do generals keep their armies?

Answer:
In their sleevies.

I laughed the first time I heard that joke. And that was the point. To surprise me. To make me laugh, or at least be amused.

But let's pretend the writer of the joke decided it should go like this:

Question:
Where do American, four-star generals, who are over the age of fifty-seven and have a good sense of humor—where do they, especially during wartimes, keep their armies?

Answer:
In their sleevies.

Huh? The joke doesn't work, does it.

Instead of priming the listener for the punch line, it has them way off thinking about other things. The only information they need to hear is information that leads them to the punch line.

Like jokes, songs can only be about one thing. Not a punch line, per se, but a surprise. A controlling idea or theme; a new way of looking at the world. All the information should point to that in some relevant way. If it doesn't, the song becomes diluted.

This is most difficult when you've come up with lines you're proud of, but then realize in the context of the entire song they don't work. A mature songwriter will get rid of them. A less-mature one will hang on to them.

This happens to me a lot. I get so zoomed in on a line or two that I forget people won't be experiencing the song under a microscope. So I have to constantly zoom in and out of my lyrics to get perspective. I play it down from the top. I take a break. I grab my yo-yo.

Ever heard the writing advice "kill your darlings"? Apply it. Nix those lines. Unnecessary information—no matter how good you think it is—is superfluous, just like all the extra info about the generals.

— On Craft —

CHECK YOUR VERB TENSE

I wrote a song in present tense the other day. I like to write in present tense because it's fun for both me and the listener. I get to use a bunch of active verbs, and the listener gets to feel like they're on a journey with me in the moment.

The bad part about this particular song was that, when finished, I realized the singer wasn't credible. I couldn't quite put my finger on it. Was it a lyrical choice, a structure problem?

It was actually a verb tense issue. The lyrics were in present tense. But the thoughts the singer was revealing wouldn't be thoughts they'd have in that moment. It'd be as if you wrote a breakup song in present tense, but also reflected on the meaning of relationships and heartache in that same moment. You wouldn't do that. You wouldn't be so philosophical in an emotional moment.

Sure, maybe there are exceptions. But I'm just saying—rule of thumb—present tense, while good for a lot of reasons, isn't as good for reflective songs. And sometimes songs that are in past tense could feel more alive and exciting in present tense.

So before you get too far into your song, establishing rhyme scheme, etc., make sure the verb tense feels right. You can test it by switching up the tense while writing. If you start the song in present tense, switch it to past, maybe even future. If the song is in past tense, try it in present. Doing so obviously makes the song feel different. But what is less obvious is how a change in tense will affect the believability of your character and the strength of your song.

— On Craft —

IT'S USUALLY THE SIMPLEST WAY

This happens to me time and time again. I want to say something clever and original. I certainly don't want to sound cliche. So I go around in circles on a particular line in a song looking for a fresh way to say something. I have to remind myself that cleverness and originality are not the only goal. Clarity is, too.

I know, like me, you don't want to sound cliche in your songs. But just remember not every line has to be full of novelty. You run the risk of trying to sound too smart. Worse, you're distracting the listener. It's Jack and Jill went up the hill. Not Jack and Jill traversed the mountainside. You don't need to sound like Shakespeare or switch into King James English. Write the way you talk, how regular people talk. If you're like me, you'll find that the best lyric is usually the simplest way of saying something.

— On Craft —

WHAT'S YOUR ANTITHESIS?

If you want your song's theme to have more impact, you need to juxtapose it with its antithesis. Why? Because life is relative. We don't know what something is until we know what it isn't. We know what night is because we've experienced day. We know what cold is because we've felt warmth.

So let's say your theme is "we're all in this together." What's the antithesis? Something along the lines of "I'm alone and there's no one here to help me."

Maybe in the verse you show one disheartened person struggling to accomplish a task on their own. They're about to give up when someone comes along to help, and then another.

Your chorus about togetherness will be much stronger because the listener will have just visualized and vicariously felt its antithesis.

— On Craft —

3 QUESTIONS TO BREAK THE CURSE OF KNOWLEDGE

My dad is an electrician. Naturally, I call him when I have an electrical problem. He'll troubleshoot with me over the phone, and I understand him for a little bit. But then he slips into jargon and electrical-speak and I have to have him explain what he means. When it comes to wiring a house, my dad has what's called the "curse of knowledge." His relationship to it is so natural, he forgets others don't share that same relationship.

As a songwriter, you have the curse of knowledge, too. You're so close to the song you're writing that it's easy to make the mistake of thinking others know what it is you're talking about. So here are three questions that will help you break the curse.

1. What's your singer's perspective?

Is your singer narrating in first person? "I went over here, I did this thing, and met with some people…" or are they in second person, "You went over there and did this thing, and met with some people…" or third person, "He went over there and did this thing and met with some people."

And what tense are they in? Is this happening in the moment, present tense? "I go over here, I do this thing, and meet with some people…" or is it in the past past? "I went over here, I did this thing, and met with some people." Or future? "I'll go over here, I'll do this thing, and meet with some people."

Your singer's perspective matters. It helps avoid verb-tense confusion for your listener. Plus there's often a perspective that will be a stronger choice than other perspectives. (Think if Bob Dylan had written "Times They Are a Changin'" in past tense.)

2. To whom are they singing?

This is related to perspective. Are they singing to a friend, an ex-lover, the world in general? It doesn't have to be explicit, but just clear enough to the listener to ground them. The sooner the better. It makes the listener's brain stop wasting calories on trying to organize the information.

3. What's your "so what?" factor?

In college, I had a creative writing professor teach me this. The "so what?" factor is a universal truth. It should ring true for everyone or most everyone. It's the subtext of your song. Yeah, you might be singing about a breakup, but you're really talking about loneliness. You might be singing about your road trip with friends, but you're really talking about togetherness and the value of community.

Side note: There are plenty of songs that don't have a "so what?" factor, but are still compelling. I'm sure you have favorite songs with no idea what they're about. But that's likely because of the delivery and expression. The emotion is authentic. The reason you like it has more to do with the artist being the songwriter and expressing their truth. So, if you're an artist and just wanting to express something in a compelling way, you might be off the hook regarding this lesson. It won't mean you'll have a good song, though. Just good art.

— On Craft —

REWRITE IT

Great lyrics and a bad melody. I once sent this combination to my publisher. They sent it right back to me and basically said, "Don't waste good lyrics on a bad melody." It hurt my feelings, but then I realized they were right. I scrapped the entire melody and rewrote it, improving the song immensely.

You can do this, too. A song doesn't need to be finished just because you think you finished it. I even think songs you've officially released can still be reworked (presuming they're not hits!).

Pull an old song out, take the best pieces of it, and make a new song. Go through songs you've written and see if they can be improved upon by a better lyric or melody.

Starting from scratch has its merits, but so does rewriting songs that aren't having an impact on anyone.

Guess what happened after Tom Douglas and Allen Shamblin decided to rewrite (multiple times) "The House that Built Me"?[1] It won CMA's Song of the Year and spent four weeks on the U.S. Billboard Hot Country Songs chart.[2]

---

[1] "The Story Behind the Song: 'The House That Built Me'," YouTube, 3 October 2016, https://www.youtube.com/watch?v=aiqKtpF3zE8&t=295s.

[2] Billboard - Miranda Lambert Chart History. https://www.billboard.com/artist/miranda-lambert/chart-history/csi/ Accessed 24 October 2023.

ON MINDSET

"Whenever my teammates ask me, 'Are you throwing today?' I tell them, 'No, I'm pitching.'"

—Adam Wainright, Major League Baseball player

— On Mindset —

HAPPY ACCIDENTS (OR ACTION-DENTS)

While painting, Bob Ross famously used to say to his viewers, "We don't make mistakes, we just have happy accidents." I want to point out something obvious: We don't have happy accidents unless we make mistakes—and you can't make mistakes if you aren't taking action.

When's the last time you had a happy accident? Maybe you took a wrong turn and ended up on a street with a house for sale. You bought it and raised a family there (big example). Maybe one day you called a friend and the friend thought you said one thing, but you'd really said a different thing. But the conversation took a turn at that point for the better (small example).

In both cases, you were doing the same thing, which is to say you were living life. You were doing something.

Action, action, action.

In almost every song I write there's a handful of happy accidents that happen in the process of writing it. Just the other day, I accidentally pressed the spacebar. My demo track started at the middle of the song, and I realized those chord changes would be really interesting at the beginning of the song.

The famous whistling in Otis Redding's "(Sittin' On) The Dock of the Bay" was him forgetting his ad-lib rap and whistling as a place holder.[1] Kurt Cobain was unaware that Teen Spirit was a deodorant brand. When he saw the graffiti a friend had written on his wall that said, "Kurt smells like teen spirit," he thought it meant

---

[1] "Inside Otis Redding's Final Masterpiece 'Sittin' on The Dock of the Bay'." Rolling Stone, https://www.rollingstone.com/music/music-features/inside-otis-reddings-final-masterpiece-sittin-on-the-dock-of-the-bay-122170/. Accessed 24 October 2023.

something deeper and wrote the song "Smells Like Teen Spirit."[1]

The best way to have more happy accidents is to do more things. Simply thinking about doing things doesn't produce happy accidents. You gotta take action.

---

[1] "Nirvana's music video Nevermind turns 20." The Guardian, https://www.theguardian.com/music/2007/jul/19/popandrock.nirvana. Accessed 24 October 2023.

— On Mindset —

IF YOU LACK LIFE EXPERIENCE

There was this scene in a cartoon my son was watching where two kids wanted to be rock stars. They started writing a song but realized they didn't have enough life experience to say much in their lyrics. So they went out and started doing a bunch of things to expedite the process. I laughed and my son asked me what was so funny.

Songs come from concepts, and concepts come from ideas. Ideas come from thoughts, and thoughts come from experiencing life. In the same way you can't have happy accidents unless you're actually doing something, you can't have compelling thoughts, ideas, or concepts without having experiences that move you in some way.

If you're young or you feel like you don't have much to say, go do something. Travel. Read a book. Climb a tree. Put yourself in a new situation. It might seem contrived, but writers do this all the time. Ron M. Persing's *Zen and the Art of Motorcycle Maintenance*. *Eat Pray Love* by Elizabeth Gilbert. Bon Iver's *For Emma, Forever Ago*. These works and countless others were written by people forcing their creative hand into giving them material. You can do that, too.

— On Mindset —

LET PEOPLE PUT YOU IN A BOX

I know you don't want to be put in a box. It feels limiting. And if you let people put you in a box with a certain label, they won't understand the breadth of what you offer, right? You're not just the catchy pop lyricist; you also write heartfelt ballads. You're not just a jazz guitarist; you're a composer who scores music for commercials.

Well, here's the thing: People are busy. Crazy busy. It doesn't mean they don't care. It just means they can't deal with too much information. If you allow them to put you in a box, it means two very great things: one, they'll remember you, and two, they'll have an entry point to go deeper.

There's this restaurant down the street. It's the "hot chicken" place. The first time I went there, guess what I was in the mood for? Yeah, hot chicken. But guess what I found out? They have an amazing craft beer selection. I went there for the obvious reason, because I'd put them in a box. But after getting me in the door, I was pleasantly surprised by their broader offerings. Instead of spending ten dollars, I spent fifteen.

Do you see what I'm getting at?

Let people put you in a box. If you do, they'll remember you. After that you can surprise and delight them with your other offerings.

— On Mindset —

IT'S LIKE NAMING A CHILD

It's easy to get excited about your half-written song. Rather than finish it, you email your verse and chorus to twenty-five friends. You just can't help yourself. That dopamine hit of validation would feel so good right now.

Well, get a grip, ok? I urge you not to share your excitement too soon. Why? It's like naming a child.

Before the baby's born you've got two choices: tell people the names you're thinking of or keep them secret.

Let's say you tell them. Sure, you'll get people who say, "I love that name!" But you'll also get people who tell you that's their dog's name. Or worse, you'll get polite nods with "Interesting." Pretty soon you're questioning every name you've ever loved. But it's your own fault. You let too many people into your creative process.

If you absolutely must share your excitement on your song early on, just ask one or two trusted friends. People who can give you enough information to make the song better, and enough encouragement to help you finish it. Go the other route and you'll invite too many voices inside your head. Pleasing all of them will be impossible.

— On Mindset —

DISCOVERING YOUR UNIQUE VOICE

If you're having trouble finding your unique songwriting voice, imagine your brain as being a giant rain barrel. The top is open. Everything you take in—experiences, reading, watching TV, whatever—is input that comes from a raincloud. The water is stored in the barrel.

Now imagine you have a bunch of spouts all over this barrel. These spouts represent your output. One spout is an email you wrote yesterday. Another spout is a text you sent to a friend. Another is a picture you took. A journal entry.

Your job as a songwriter is to identify all the spouts on your barrel that act as your natural outputs. These are the "you" everybody already knows. The kinds of photos you take, you take them for a reason. The kinds of emails and texts you write, you have a way you do that—things you always say or a style you have. Opinions you speak up about.

Your unique songwriting voice is really just a continuation of the stuff you're already doing, but simply editing it down and changing its form. There's no need to go out looking for it because it's already in you. The barrel and spouts metaphor can help you home in on it.

— On Mindset —

IS THIS SONG ANY GOOD?

Is this song any good? That's a question songwriters ask themselves a lot. But "good" is subjective. What's less subjective is knowing whether your song is remarkable.

Remarkable is the thing you're after as a songwriter. What do I mean by "remarkable"? I mean someone, of their own volition, remarking about your song. This can't be if you're asking for feedback. That doesn't count. It is somebody reaching out to you in an email or coming up to you after a show. It could be someone messaging you on social media. However they do it, the person is going out of their way to say your song was meaningful to them.

Remarkable is important because you can actually quantify it. Pay attention to this metric when trying out new material. Why? Think about what it takes for someone to get to the point where they remark on your song. First, they have to have taken the time to listen. Second, they listened closely enough to have been impacted by the song. Third, your song has stuck in this person's mind and heart. Fourth, they take action to thank you—they remark. That's a significant impact and a useful metric or tool to show you which songs resonate. If it resonates with one person, it will likely resonate with many.

Put the songs people remark on in your "remarkable" folder. These songs, regardless of how you feel about them, are worth spending more time on. Play them live more often. If unreleased, release them.

— On Mindset —

WHAT'S THE BIGGER TRUTH?

Your job as a songwriter is not to simply relay a story as it actually happened. Sure, there are great real-life stories out there, but for the most part they need to be adjusted or embellished for a bigger truth.

Let me give you an example of what I'm talking about.

In a song of mine called "Small Town," I sing:

> *My dad said,*
> *"Kids, listen to your mother,*
> *Treat her like you love her,*
> *Look out for each other.*
> *Someday soon,*
> *When you have family,*
> *You will know what I mean,*
> *You will know what I mean."*

Now, did my dad actually say those words? No. I made them up. But did he say those words in the way he lived his life? Yes, absolutely. And that's the bigger truth. That's the message he delivered. Had I only been concerned about actual facts the lyrics would have gone something like:

> *My dad said,*
> *Nothing much hardly ever,*
> *But he bought my mom flowers,*
> *Attended all of our sporting events,*
> *Got up and went to work everyday.*

As a songwriter, I would have put my listeners through a lot of awkward pain to listen to those lyrics being sung. It made more sense to have my dad say things I made up; like he was sitting us kids down and distilling his life into a few words.

Don't just relay facts. You're not a reporter, you're a songwriter. Be less concerned with actual events to help your listeners see a bigger truth.

— On Mindset —

BE UNORIGINAL

I loved the book *Steal Like an Artist* by Austin Kleon. If you haven't already read it, please use it as a deep dive into the below topic. For now, I'm going to give you a bite-sized songwriting version.

Here we go:

A rookie mistake in songwriting is thinking you have to be original.

You don't.

Well, not really.

Start by thinking of your favorite song, unless that song is "Bohemian Rhapsody," "The Long and Winding Road," or some other complicated masterpiece. Choose a song that's simple, but still mysterious enough that you have to figure out how to play and sing it.

At the time I started writing, my favorite song was "Glory Bound" by Martin Sexton. I knew the basic chords he was playing on guitar, but there was a lot I didn't know. Figuring it out helped me have "ah-ha" moments; tiny breakthroughs that made me think about the guitar differently. I learned to put my hands in new positions and use unconventional voicings. And singing over those voicings helped me develop phrasing techniques that I wouldn't have otherwise come up with. It unlocked new worlds.

So, step one, learn your favorite simple song.

Step two? Take everything you've learned and transfer the parts you like most onto your own song. I'll give you an example.

One of the first songs I wrote after learning "Glory Bound" is a song called "Melody." If you A/B "Glory Bound" and "Melody" you won't hear a whole lot of similarity, but you'll sense something familiar. That's because the phrasing of the melody, the pace of the guitar, the plucking and hits on the fretboard—they're all heavily influenced by Martin Sexton.

Don't think you have to be original. Nobody's original. We're all stealing from our influences, sprinkling in our own take on things, and combining it with our life experiences. The end result is a wonderful collage that's as original as anything can be.

Side note: I'm speaking more to you writers who become paralyzed by the fear of being unoriginal. It keeps you from writing. I hope it goes without saying that I'm not talking about plagiarizing. I also hope it goes without saying that you should always try to be as original as you can be. Follow your intuition, your curiosity. Dig deep into your soul. Push yourself. Mostly, though, have fun.

— On Mindset —

BORING LIFE IS INTERESTING

If you're like me, you probably don't think your life is all that interesting. You wake up, have breakfast. Go to work. Come home, hang with the family. Maybe see some friends or watch TV. Go to bed.

On the surface, that's not so interesting. But if you were to zoom in on one specific thing—even something fairly mundane—I bet you could find something surprisingly interesting.

Let's take this morning, for example. I was in a hurry to get the kids to school. But I made sure to have my coffee. I prefer it without cream or sugar. I like to taste the beans. The beans this morning were from Guatemala. "Notes of grapes and chocolate" it said on the packaging. I poured it into my favorite porcelain mug. It has the perfect thickness with an ergonomic lip. The cup is only about six ounces. I like smaller mugs so the coffee doesn't get cold.

I could go on about my morning coffee for a long time. The more zoomed in I get, the more details come out. And the more details that come out, the more I catch little paradoxes and things of interest. The fact that I'm in a hurry to get the kids to school, but the coffee slows me down. I sip it. I enjoy it. I could write a song called "Morning Coffee." Maybe it's a song about trying not to hurry my life away, even in the midst of household chaos.

What's the lesson here? Mine your boring life. There's gold in there!

— On Mindset —

FAIRY DUST AND WORK ETHIC

Sometimes when I'm on a walk, I'll come to an intersection and a kind driver will wave for me to go ahead. I wave back and start walking. But I don't walk normally; I pick up the pace as a courtesy. They might not want me to rush, but that's beside the point. The point is I'm acknowledging their generosity with a little extra effort.

Songwriting is like that. It's both mystery and craft. You're stuck at a crosswalk with heavy traffic, but a kind driver says, "Here you go, I see you. Let me make this a little easier on you."

A kind driver is the fairy dust. Something you didn't earn; it was given to you. An old memory out of nowhere, or seeing something random outside your window.

The hustle of getting across the intersection is work ethic. It's on you to make the appropriate effort.

When inspiration and mystery hit you, treat them like gifts. Say thank you. How? Record the idea on your phone. Write down that thought that occurred. Redo the bridge section of that one song that wasn't quite working.

Most of all, receive the gifts and respond in kind with hustle in your step. If you're like me, you'll find that the more you do, the more kind drivers you meet.

— On Mindset —

WRITE WHAT YOU DON'T KNOW

Everyone says to write what you know. There's a lot of truth to that advice. You'll have more confidence and authority, plus you'll be pulling from a deeper well. But even if you write about what you know, you're not going to know everything.

For example, yesterday I was trying to write a song about boats. I've spent a lot of my life on boats. Worked on them, driven them, paddled them, fished in them. But even so, as I was writing I realized I didn't know some of the terminology or technical language.

At that point I could have said to myself, "Well, I don't want to be a boat poser, so I guess I'll stop writing about boats." But instead I went where I always go: Wikipedia. I read about boats for a while, jotting down terms and other words I thought could be handy.

You can do this, too. You're not cheating. You're not posing. Think of it like gardening. Maybe you know zilch about it. But you've certainly eaten fruits and vegetables. And you've played in the dirt before.

— On Mindset —

MAKE IT EASY

Recently my wife Heidi started leaving a plate of fresh fruit on the counter. Everything's washed, peeled, sliced, and arranged beautifully on a plate. I'll find myself walking past and grabbing an apple slice or handful of grapes. Our kids eat more fruit now, too. Why? Heidi knew our family needed more fiber in our diet. So, quite brilliantly, she made fiber extremely easy to consume. She removed all the resistance besides picking it up and putting it in our mouths.

Like eating healthier, you can make songwriting a more regular activity by removing resistance. How do you do that? Well, if I come to your house and see that your guitar is in its case under your bed—that's a problem. Do you know what has to happen between you saying, "Time to write a song" and actually doing it? Literally getting on your hands and knees, pulling the case out, unbuckling all the straps, shoving the empty case somewhere, finding a spot to sit down. We haven't even talked about tuning or finding a pen and paper.

You know where my guitar is right now? It's two feet to my right. Within an arm's reach. That's how little I trust myself to write a song with any degree of resistance. So I make it as easy as possible. Pen and paper out. Guitar tuned, leaning somewhere close.

Even in a chaotic house like mine with four wild boys bouncing off the walls, it's possible. For a while I turned my son's closet into a writing room. He couldn't sleep unless someone was in the room with him. So I wrote in his closet with the door open while he drifted off to sleep.

It's possible. Get creative to remove as much resistance as you can.

— On Mindset —

UPDATE YOUR BRAIN'S OPERATING SYSTEM

Every so often I get an iPhone update. I hate updates at first because I don't like change. Why did they have to do another update? The look is only slightly different; there's a few new features, but was it worth the bother?

After a few days the answer is almost always yes. The changes weren't just changes; they were improvements. They may have been small, but they made using the device better or easier in some way.

What are you doing to continually update your own operating system as a songwriter? If you're like me, you don't like change, but you do desire improvement. And it's easy to confuse the two.

Improvement is simply growth over time. It doesn't mean you suddenly need to start writing songs in a different style or quit the guitar and move to the melodica. Improvement means you keep track of the times you think, "Huh, I really like that sound" or "the way she sang that lyric was unexpected" and then incorporate elements of that in your own work.

When you index those thoughts in your brain or notes, you update your operating system. Your songwriting improves and becomes more enjoyable and user friendly.

— On Mindset —

PAINT WITH THE BRUSHES YOU HAVE

I'm currently learning to paint. I keep thinking if I buy a better brush or get some different paper, I'll get better faster. Truth is, those are just excuses for not painting.

Every time I paint, I learn more about painting than watching twenty YouTube tutorials and reading a book about painting. Don't get me wrong, added instruction is helpful, but it's essentially worthless without me actually painting.

As for songwriting, whatever you have to start with will work. You don't need anything, really. To write a song, you need your thoughts. Those thoughts turn into ideas, and those ideas eventually turn into concepts that you can organize with nothing other than a working brain and your singing voice.

Sure, pen and paper, an instrument, a basic understanding of theory (this book!)—all of that is helpful, but not necessary.

No more excuses. Write with whatever you've got. Paint with the brushes you have.

— On Mindset —

TWO IS ONE

The Navy SEALs have a saying, "Two is one and one is none." It's all about planning and having a backup plan. If you don't have a backup plan, you don't have a plan because inevitably things will go wrong. Let's say you want to wake up tomorrow at 6 AM. For the SEALs, setting an alarm clock isn't a plan. Setting an alarm clock and a backup alarm clock is a plan.

It makes me think about how important it is to have a plan and backup plan for capturing your song ideas. Just last night I was in bed and had an idea. I usually keep my ideas in my Notes app, but I had already plugged my iPhone into the wall in the bathroom, because I don't like to sleep with my phone near me. For that reason, I usually have a stack of index cards on the night stand for song ideas. But when I looked to the nightstand, there wasn't a pen. I saw I'd forgotten to put one back. I gave up and resorted to "I'll try to remember tomorrow." Guess what? It didn't work.

Have a plan and a backup plan like Navy SEALs do. Who knows, maybe your idea will lead to a hit song. But the surefire way to make sure it doesn't is to not remember it.

— On Mindset —

THE CALENDAR HACK

First of all, do you keep a calendar? Do you stick with it? Is "songwriting" on there?

Every morning at the same time each day "solo songwriting" is written on my calendar. I almost never write songs just because I feel like it. I do it because it's on my calendar.

You might be thinking, "That seems so Type A. What about the muse, the inspiration, all the mysterious stuff about songwriting?" In my experience, muses tend to keep a tighter schedule when I do. I imagine them saying among themselves, "Hey, gang. Espe's really showing up, let's make sure we show up, too."

Sure, they don't show up everyday. But when they do, I'm more prepared to connect. It's like I'm standing in the batter's box with my bat ready. I'm not in the dugout chewing bubble gum or still driving to the ball field.

But while I'm on the subject, let me ask you: What came first, the inspiration or sitting down to write? The chicken or the egg?

Yes. Neither. And both!

We assume people are in a good mood when we hear them start to whistle. But that's not always the case. You can whistle to put yourself in a good mood. You can smile to make yourself feel happier. And the same is true with songwriting. You can show up without being inspired and find yourself becoming incredibly motivated.

Your calendar helps make that happen. It's your cue to start whistling.

ON DEALING WITH YOUR INNER CRITIC

"Espe, you suck."

—This kid from high school, who I still think about sometimes

— On Dealing with Your Inner Critic —

BEFORE ANYONE HURTS YOUR FEELINGS

A great movie writer and director was reportedly heard telling a group of students that he likes to write early in the morning before anyone has hurt his feelings.

Think about that for a second.

There is so much truth in that one little tip that I've tried to abide by it since hearing it years ago. In fact, I'm doing it right now. It's 8 AM. My confidence is high. I'm typing with purpose, without questioning every word.

Because I know at some point today, someone will say something or I'll do something that will hijack my brain. With a hijacked brain it's difficult to be creative. I turn into what I call the Delete Monster, where I start trashing everything I've created up until that point in the day. It's usually around 3 PM.

I have a rule now that I don't delete anything after 1pm. I know my brain is fatigued by then or soon thereafter. I try to get all my writing done early.

Try it out. Write before you check social media and email. Before you turn on the radio or converse with anyone. I bet you'll discover the words come easier and you'll stave off the Delete Monster.

— On Dealing with Your Inner Critic —
5-4-3-2-1

Even after writing hundreds and hundreds of songs, it still happens every time. Here's the scenario: I've just finished a song. I attach it to an email and compose a message to my publisher. But before I hit "send" I pause. I question the song. Is it good enough? Is it even worth their time? What if they laugh at me? Worse, what if they are completely indifferent?

I spiral into other areas of my life. What am I doing? Am I even a songwriter? I soon find myself online looking for job openings at Best Buy and Home Depot. Can I feed my family on $11 an hour?

I finally I shake myself out of it, "Come on, Espe, get yourself together, man!"

I count down 5-4-3-2-1 and hit "send."

As creative people, sharing our work is difficult because we want people to affirm it, and ultimately affirm us. But the reality is you've already affirmed your work by creating it and getting it to this point. You certainly didn't spend all that time on it because you think it's crap, right?

So when in doubt—which will likely be often—use that knowledge to get to the next part: sharing your work. Your song doesn't count unless you do that. Why? Because part of the reason we write songs is to make a connection with others—to help both them and us feel less alone in the world.

That doesn't happen unless we hit the "send."

— On Dealing with Your Inner Critic —

USE YOUR JEALOUSY FOR GOOD

Jealously. It's bound to happen as a songwriter. Someone has written something you wish you had. Someone is getting the praise you think you deserve. Then you feel bad about feeling this way, which leads to feeling worse until you begin stress-eating Cheetos.

What I recommend for the long term is therapy. Like me, you probably have lots of inner work that needs to be done and it's going to be a long haul.

But for the short term, here's a tool that's actually quite useful when you experience songwriting jealousy.

Tell the person you're jealous of that you're jealous of them for writing that song. Go ahead, email them or even post a comment on their social media feed for everyone to see.

One, it's the truth. And, two, that's the greatest compliment you can give a songwriter. To tell them you wish you'd written something they wrote. It's a win-win.

Telling them this will make them feel great. But it will also help you feel less bad. Moreover, it will humanize the person you envy after you've mentally turned them into an evil villain. That was your jealousy talking; they are not in fact evil…probably.

And remember what I said about therapy? I wasn't joking.

— On Dealing with Your Inner Critic —

NERVOUS IS NORMAL

No matter how many times I write a song, whether alone or collaborating, I'm always a bit nervous. What if I can't finish the song? What if the other writer hates my ideas? What if I die? Well, not usually that last one, but sometimes it feels that way.

One day I confessed this to my songwriter friend. He's written numerous hits, so I was surprised when he said he feels the same. Every time he writes a song. Success hadn't changed any of it. If anything, there was added pressure to sustain the success, and a hit songwriter can't guarantee another hit song. It doesn't work that way.

It's ok to be nervous, because songwriting isn't predictable. The reason you and I write songs isn't because we know that two plus two equals four. We write songs because we have no idea what might happen on any particular day. It's a constant charting of the unknown; creating something out of nothing.

So just show up anyway. Oftentimes, showing up is half the battle.

— On Dealing with Your Inner Critic —

BE A CHARACTER WE'D LOVE IN A MOVIE

At some point you're going to want someone to say something nice about your songs. Anything. You might think you're one of those people who doesn't care what anyone else thinks. I sure hope you're right. All the rest of us are slaves to other people's opinions. At least a little bit.

I remember the first time I had to go out soliciting blurbs for my first album. I didn't know anyone. I wanted somebody who sounded like a somebody to say, "Best album ever…the next Bob Dylan!" But I couldn't find anybody who would say that without me blackmailing them. Unfortunately, I wanted it to be genuine.

The hard part about this vulnerable period of time is being in mid air. You've already jumped. You've given a piece of your heartfelt-self to the world. And so you're just falling and waiting.

What's required here is some good old fashioned hope and patience. That's step one.

Step two? I've found it's best not to have nothing to do after you've released a project into the world. You will ring your fingers until the skin comes off. You will hate everybody for not loving your work as much as you think they should. You will go online and it will seem like everybody else is having more success than you. Don't be that person. Get busy with something, anything.

The last thing, and probably the most helpful step, is to imagine yourself as the character in a movie. First, imagine the movie playing out in the way you hoped it would when you first released your songs. The back of the movie cover reads, "Kid from small town writes songs. Everybody loves them and he becomes famous." That would be the worst movie ever made. Nobody wants to see that movie. Where's the hero's journey?

It would be better if it reads, "Kid from small town heads for the big city with a handful of songs. Nobody pays any attention, until one day...."

That's a better movie.

But the "nobody pays any attention" part seems long. And it can be. Regardless it's the scene you're in. Realize it. Get through it with as much dignity as you can. Be the character in a movie who, when the going gets tough, the audience sympathizes and keeps rooting for you.

— On Dealing with Your Inner Critic —

SHUSHING

Songwriting is mostly shushing. You have to shush people in your head for a good hour or two.

"Dumb idea," says one.

"Shush!" you say.

"Stupid," says another.

"Shush."

There are about fifteen or so people badmouthing you and they look like your mom and dad. They look like the kid who sat behind you in math class and stuck things on the back of your shirt. They look like your relatives, people who you think would say, "That's not really who you are." Or "That didn't really happen to you. I know who you are."

And you'd think that once you become a published songwriter the validation of a paycheck for your songs would be the ultimate shush. But it isn't. The voices come back and you gotta keep shushing.

The good news is there's another voice that's always there as well, except it's just whispering rather than shouting like all the others. And you've gotta tell everybody else, "Stop! From now on you have to raise your hand to speak. Because I can't hear my soft-spoken friend!"

And then it gets a little better.

But like a class of third-graders, they forget and you have to remind them all again the next day.

Side note: One of my favorite books on creative writing is by Anne Lamott called *Bird by Bird*. Read the whole thing, but particularly her chapter called "Radio Station KFKD."

— On Dealing with Your Inner Critic —

DOUBTING THE VISION

Somewhere in the middle of your song you're going to doubt yourself. It's going to feel like you must have been wrong; like the vision you had when you started was way off. But don't give up and go eat ice cream just yet. Reserve final judgement until after you've finished the process.

Finishing the process is the only way I know how to honor and defend the vision. Whether it's good or not is irrelevant. That's not really for you, the artist and songwriter, to decide.

A few days ago I was in the middle of a recording session. I started doubting everything I was doing. I was hoping a legitimate excuse to quit would fall in my lap. Maybe my wife would call and say a pipe had burst, or maybe the IRS would audit me. I'd be thrilled.

But I knew I had to keep going. I had to record the percussion and final vocals to see the vision through.

The end result? In my opinion, it wasn't great. But you know what? My publisher loved it, and so did others.

As creative people, there's a reason why we get so excited about an idea, something so abstract but something we so clearly see in our mind's eye. Honor your vision by finishing the process.

— On Dealing with Your Inner Critic —

WHY DISAPPOINTMENT IS YOUR FRIEND

As mentioned earlier, I started learning how to paint watercolor. I've been watching all these YouTube videos on technique, mixing paint, tonal value studies, among other things. And as I'm watching, I can picture myself doing the same thing the instructor is doing. It's clear to me in that moment, so effortless.

Then I grab my paints and brushes and begin. I concentrate and work at it for an hour or so. The only problem is that by the end I'm so freaking disappointed with the result that I want to eat ice cream for the rest of my life.

Yesterday I painted a landscape. Large sky, mountains, a little farm. It looked like something Bob Ross might paint … if someone had blindfolded him and made him use his toes.

The small part of me that wasn't disappointed was only because of one thing: I noticed I'd improved a little from my last painting. (The gradation in my sky looked half decent!)

If you want to get better at songwriting, get comfortable with disappointment. Actually, start thinking of disappointment as your friend. It's a gift that reminds you that you're taking action. You're trying. Most people who want to write a song won't do it. Being disappointed with a song is still light years ahead of those people who want to write a song, but haven't taken action.

Plus, if you and your new buddy Disappointment meet up often, you'll notice that one percent of improvement adds up over time. Soon the scale will be tipping in your favor. From disappointment to pride. I'm hoping by this time next year, I'll have a watercolor painting that at least looks like Bob Ross took the blindfold off!

— On Dealing with Your Inner Critic —

IMPOSTER SYNDROME

Imposter syndrome is what I'm feeling right now as I'm writing about songwriting. "Who are you to think you can say anything about songwriting? There's plenty of people better than you, more qualified than you who should be doing it and have already done it. Plus, you're a terrible speller!"

The thing is, I've grown accustomed to imposter syndrome for so long now it feels like a familiar stranger. Somebody I wave to every time I sit down to write. He sits over there in the corner shouting obscenities like a drunk at the bus stop.

And much like the chapters on shushing and disappointment, imposter syndrome doesn't seem to entirely go away. It's just a part of the deal.

So don't feel bad about having it. It's normal. Sure, maybe you're faking it a little bit, but so are we all. Just do your best work and try to help others.

ON COWRITING

"A cord of three strands is not quickly broken."

—Ecclesiastes 4:12

— On Cowriting —

WHAT'S COWRITING?

Have you ever watched the TV show *House*? It's about a brilliant but abrasive doctor who is masterful at solving difficult-to-diagnose cases. In the show, Dr. House and his team of doctors hold meetings. In the room, there's a whiteboard, and House paces, holding a marker while his team offers possible diagnoses. Lupus? No. Thrombosis? No. Keep going. "Talk," House says. Cavernous angioma? Et cetera, et cetera.

Everyone is throwing out ideas, and House writes everything down on the whiteboard, connecting dots. They get closer, then further away until, after trial and error and testing, and sometimes getting it wrong, they figure out what it is: gold sodium thiomalate poisoning.

Or whatever.

This is cowriting. It's a continuous back-and-forth, trying to solve a problem. The problem, of course, isn't diagnosing a disease. It's figuring out what the song is about, why it matters, and how to tell the story in a way that resonates.

In the end, your diagnosis is encompassed by a title: "Will You Still Love Me Tomorrow," "The Long and Winding Road" – not unlike gold sodium thiomalate poisoning.

— On Cowriting —

AVOIDING THE AWKWARD START

Cowriting is a strange activity if you've never done it before. Especially with someone new. But here's something that helps me ease into the write without it feeling too awkward.

As you're getting to know each other, keep track of words and phrases that stick out. Interesting topics. You don't have to write it down, but just be aware.

After you've been chatting for a bit, rather than saying, "Ok, what should we write about?" you can mention the things you've been keeping track of. Words, phrases, interesting paradoxes.

Why do this? It's less jarring and more natural. And it makes everything you've talked about so far a part of the cowrite. It's like the conversation was the onramp, and now you can easily merge onto the highway. It saves you time and headspace.

The other day I was in a session. My cowriter and his wife had just had their first baby. We were talking about his new life of being a parent. After we had chatted for a while, what do you think we naturally wrote? A heavy metal banger?

No, a lullaby.

Try starting your cowriting session from the minute you say, "Hi, nice to meet you." It'll help guide you toward a more natural collaboration and avoid the awkward start.

— On Cowriting —

COMMITMENT ISSUES

I was in a cowriting session the other day with a friend. She and I both presented some song ideas. We dissected each and looked at what was interesting, their strengths and weaknesses.

The first one could go in this direction. It could be about this topic or that topic. The subtext would be about such and such. This other song idea could maybe be about this other topic. The third song idea? Well, it had a great title, it would be a fun title to sing.

They were all great ideas and excited us for different reasons. But we kept going on like this for an hour, burning through valuable writing energy and headspace.

Brass tacks? We didn't write a song that day.

It was a classic case of commitment issues.

So much of songwriting is throwing caution to the wind, and going for it—saying yes to your idea and sticking with it to the end. It's hard to let go of other thoughts and ideas, the potential of "what could be." But at the end of the day, an idea turned into a song is better than three ideas living in abstraction.

Try to make a point of committing within the first twenty minutes of a collaboration (after all the pleasantries, etc.). The only litmus test should be whether the idea excites you and your cowriter. That way you'll save your brain calories on the thing that really matters: turning the idea into a song.

— On Cowriting —

WANTED: DUMB IDEAS

Sometimes when you're writing you'll have an idea that seems dumb. I notice this a lot more when I'm cowriting. In these scenarios it's harder to chase the idea because I have a witness to my potential stupidity.

Still, the idea fairy tapped on my shoulder. So I find it helpful to use phrases like, "Can we try something?" or "This might be stupid, but…" or "Do you mind if we turn over this stone? It might be nothing, but…"

Phrases like this give you some freedom to sound stupid, but also to honor the idea, potentially moving the song in a direction that takes it to new heights.

Let me give you an example.

One time I was in a cowriting session and I kept hearing the phrase "Sunday night in Chinatown." It seemed completely random, so I kept it to myself for half the session. Finally, I gave up and said, "You know, this might sound stupid, but I keep hearing this phrase right here at the end of the chorus."

Guess what? My writing partner didn't think it was stupid. He loved it. It made him think of imagery and ideas he might not otherwise have accessed. And the song was significantly altered. The title? "Sunday Night in Chinatown."

Side note: Someday you'll become more confident and you'll surround yourself with cowriters you love and trust. You won't have to be so worried about sounding stupid. Till then, these phrases might come in handy. Also, if anyone *does* make you feel like an idiot, dump 'em. Life's too short. Find cowriters who bring out the best in you.

— On Cowriting —

HOW TO BE MY SUBSTITUTE COWRITER

The following chapter was initially a blog post I wrote to give a humorous but accurate glimpse into a typical cowriting session. I thought the best way to do that was to pretend the reader was going to be my substitute cowriter while I was away on a business trip.

All right, thanks for filling in for me. I know you might not have cowritten a song, let alone written a song before, but you're all I've got. Don't worry, I'm going to show you exactly what to do, ok?

First off, cowrites almost invariably start at 11 AM. Partly because Nashville is structured around family, school, and staying up late attending gigs. Sessions happen anywhere and everywhere —Music Row, publishers' offices, living rooms, home studios. I'm fortunate to have a writing space and studio in my backyard. So most cowriters will come to you when you're subbing.

I know I said cowrites start at 11 AM, but what I meant was 11:15 or 11:30. Songwriters are almost never on time. Try not to judge them too harshly. After all, the only traffic you're going to brave is the backyard squirrels.

So very loosely around 11am you will see a stranger pull into the driveway. They have either Uber'ed or driven themselves. You'll be somewhat familiar with this stranger because weeks prior my publisher will have sent you samples of their work. If you're like me, there's a seventy-five percent chance you will have googled them or stalked them on social media. It's nice to know you have a few friends in common. It's nice to know their google results didn't produce an FBI alert.

Lead them into the kitchen and make them a pour-over coffee. Ask about where they're from and what they've been up to recently. Try not to let on that you know most of this already because you've scrolled their social media feeds. The goal here is just to make them feel comfortable.

You should then open the backdoor and begin walking to the studio. They will probably mention my wife Heidi's garden and that they've always wanted to garden. Please tell them they should. Life is short. And the Internet or Heidi will answer any questions they have.

Once in the studio, you'll continue your conversation, sipping coffee. At some point, somebody has to signal that they want to start writing a song. A person putting on their coat at a restaurant suggests it's time to go. My go-to signal is to grab my Martin acoustic guitar off the wall and begin plucking a few strings like I've just sat down at Guitar Center.

I should mention here that cowriting is all about trust. If it doesn't feel like you've established enough, then the conversation can go longer. I've had cowriters just want to get coffee first before they decide to write at a future date. I've had artists talk for two hours before they sing a note. It just depends. Be prepared to go out into the wilderness and do trust falls.

While cowriting, remember what your third-grade teacher told you about the classroom: There are no dumb questions, no dumb ideas. That's true in a cowriting session. In fact, the only dumb idea is to make your cowriter feel like their idea is dumb. If you make them feel this way you'll regret it. You will notice the faucet closing. What do I mean by "faucet"? I like to affectionately think of my cowriter as the loveliest faucet in all of Home Depot. Less affectionately I consider myself one of those orange, five-gallon empty buckets in dire need of water. I don't really care about the quality of the water. I just need to fill up the bucket. We can filter the water later. A cowriter who feels dumb only drips. No, don't be disingenuous. You don't have to pretend all their ideas are brilliant. Just use common sense.

Once the first verse and chorus are completed, you'll experience a temptation to pat yourself on the back more than you deserve. Yes, appropriate amounts of back patting are fine, but too much and you won't finish the song. A half-written song is similar to an episode of home improvement show on HGTV. Except in this episode, while the host is doing the big reveal to the excited homeowner, right after they've toured the living room and kitchen, they come to the back half of the house. And it's still still in shambles. There's a drywall guy sitting on the floor eating a ham sandwich.

So, at this half-written song intersection, you have a couple of options: go to lunch or don't go to lunch. There's a benefit to both, but each has its own perils.

If you go to lunch, I suggest you go to one of my favorite restaurants, El Fuego. I recommend the "Burritos East," but everything on the menu is good.

The problem is, after you've finished this delicious meal that's now made you loosen your belt buckle, you'll lack motivation to craft the final words and melodies needed back at the Half-Written Song Ranch. In fact, the only motivation you'll feel is to hibernate.

Option two? Well, if you avoid lunch, you will likely finish the song. The problem is your grumbling stomach will reach a decibel hard to ignore. A few snacks might tame it, sure, but you'll still hear the little monsters. Plus, the microphones will pick them up on the demo you're about to record (more on that in a second).

Whatever you decide, please just muster the strength to write another verse or two, and a bridge if need be.

When the song is finished, and if your cowriter is the singer, record them singing a scratch vocal after you've laid down a rhythm guitar or piano track. That way you can later record other instruments and play around with the direction the recorded song might go.

You're about done now. It's time for goodbyes. I should warn you, this part is a bit strange, but I've gotten used to it over time. Cowriting a song is the get-to-know-you equivalent of five coffee dates. If you get coffee with a stranger five times, they are no longer a stranger but a dear friend. This is what you'll feel with your cowriter. Should they need anything in the future, you will be there for them. Sending Christmas cards, remembering birthdays and other special occasions won't be out of line. But asking them to be your child's godparent probably is. Remember, you've really only known this person for about five hours.

Give your cowriter a hug unless they're from the Midwest or Canada, then a handshake will do just fine or a farewell that lasts about seventeen minutes. Tell them you'll work on the demo and send it to them in the coming days.

At this point, my kids will want you to come inside the house and play "Monster." This just means you crawl around the house on all fours and let them jump on you, but we can get into those instructions at another time.

Thanks for doing this, and if you have any questions don't hesitate to ask.

—Aaron

ON MUSIC CITY AND THE INDUSTRY

"I guess if we're in it for the money, there are probably a lot easier ways of making it."

—My wife and me, about every six months

— On Music City and the Industry —

SHOULD YOU MOVE TO NASHVILLE?

I'm often asked by songwriters whether or not they should move to Nashville. I remember asking my Nashville songwriter friends the same question when I lived in Denver. What they (and I) were really asking was, "Do you think I have what it takes?"

As I'm writing this, I've lived in Nashville for ten years. I've watched people come and go. Dreams realized; dreams crushed. The thing about both cases is each person became a better songwriter by being here. Any writer who's been here for a while will tell you the same.

If you want to become a better songwriter, I recommend moving to Nashville. You might already be incredibly talented. If so, your talent will likely be recognized and you'll become an even stronger force by being here.

But like most of us, you might find out how bad at writing you really are, and moving here will be a wakeup call. The bar is higher. The stakes are higher. It's like an Olympic training ground for songwriters. You can't be around that environment and not improve.

If you love songwriting, then becoming a better writer is its own reward. Moving to Nashville will be worth it. If you're moving to become rich and famous, odds are you'll be disappointed.

A note of caution: If you move here, you will constantly deal with comparison syndrome. Especially at the beginning. It won't be easy. There are so many great writers. But once you learn to glean from them instead of compare yourself to them, it will get easier. You'll find yourself loving the culture instead of resenting it.

— On Music City and the Industry —

HANG WITH YOUR HIGH SCHOOL CLASSMATES

People often get to Nashville and think, "If I could just write with this person or that person, then I'd make it." But the truth is, if you just hang with your high school class you'll likely be fine. What do I mean by "high school class"?

I like to think of each year in Nashville as having a new high school class. This year saw a brand new class of freshman. They are all experiencing similar problems—How do I meet people? What's the best venue to try and play at? What's a publishing deal? How do I get one?

Try to connect with as many of your "classmates" as you can. In five years, you'll be astonished at the number of connections you have and how established in the community you are. Many of you will be experiencing success. And its a shared success. You'll be in the mix. Those relationships are what will bring you more work and opportunities.

I'm not saying that you don't ever hang out with upperclassmen (forgive the metaphor). I'm just saying that it's easier to "get in" with people who are in your class. So start there, keep doing good work, and be patient.

— On Music City and the Industry —

CHOOSING YOUR PATH

When I first moved to Music City, I wasn't sure what I wanted to do. Did I want to try my hand at country music? Was I trying to become a producer? Did I want to collaborate for my own artist projects? I wasn't sure. Partly because I didn't know what my options were exactly. As the saying goes, "you don't know what you don't know."

So I found it extremely helpful to say yes to everything. Saying yes to everything—an opportunity to write with this person or that person, try produce a genre outside my comfort zone, play at a venue for two people, get coffee with so and so—all of these were like mini job experiences. They taught me what I was good at, what I wasn't good at, and what I wanted to learn more about. I began to understand more fully the different aspects involved in "doing music."

If you're not sure what you want to do, say yes to everything. It's the fastest way to discover a path worth focusing on that could lead to your career.

— On Music City and the Industry —

SEE YOURSELF AS A SMALL BUSINESS

Want to know one of the main reasons songwriters make it in the music industry? They see themselves as a small business. They know what problem they solve.

It's a tough lesson and one I struggled with for a long time. I just wanted people to like my music and pay me enough so I didn't have to work a real job. I didn't want to think about business. (That's why I avoided all those classes in high school and college!)

But the fact is, songwriters, like any good business, solve a particular problem. A plumbing company will fix your broken pipe. A fast food joint will solve your need for cheap food on the go. Until you know what problem you solve as a songwriter, you're at a huge disadvantage.

When I first moved to Nashville, I thought I could just write good songs across all genres, make the charts, and get paid. But that didn't work. Then I started to understand that my value wasn't in being a songwriter at large, it was in bringing down-to-earth lyrics with emotional, hopeful messages. As soon as I realized that, it made everything easier. I knew what my role was in collaborations. I knew what songs to release that would have a better shot at success. My small business grew because people knew what product I offered and I knew how to deliver it.

Don't get me wrong, that didn't mean I stopped exploring new areas. It didn't mean I restricted myself to only emotional-hopeful songs. It just meant that I knew what my core offer was. That was home base. And I could stretch out from there.

See yourself as a small business owner and figure out what problem you solve. Are you the person who is great at beats and strong hooks? Are you a really great hang, and people love having you in the writing room for morale? Maybe you're the songwriter who really "gets" the vernacular of modern country music.

If you're unsure of what problem you solve, try everything, much like I did when I when I first moved to Nashville (refer to last chapter). It will become clearer with each session you're in, with each song you write.

— On Music City and the Industry —

WHAT'S YOUR 80/20?

I've never been good at math. I quit my calculus class with Mr. Wensloff to join the show choir. Had I paid more attention, I would've learned this lesson sooner. In fact, you probably already know it.

Have you ever heard of the Pareto principle? Here is the basic rundown and why you should remember it.

The Pareto principle states that about 80 percent of output comes from roughly 20 percent of input. And this is applies to many situations. For example, let's say you've got 100 tomato seeds and you plant them this summer. The vast majority (80 percent) of your harvest will likely come from only about 20 seeds.

After a few summers, smart gardeners begin to look at the types of seeds that seem to produce the most. They ask, what variety are they? Did I water these more? Did I plant them at a different depth? Did they receive more sunlight? By asking these questions they can adjust their future input—how and where they plant, how much water, etc.—on the most important tasks which will likely produce even more tomatoes.

Why is this important to you as a songwriter?

For one, it sets a realistic expectation. If you write 100 songs, only 20 will likely do anything—whether that's praise from listeners or earning income. If you release an album of 10 songs expect people to really like only two, and about 80 percent of your earnings will come from those two.

Now, after you've released music for a while and you want to play the numbers game (which isn't for everyone), act like the smart gardener with the tomatoes. Put the songs that perform well under a microscope and analyze why they might have done well. Some of the reasons are serendipitous, sure. But some might not be. Are there common threads? Maybe the songs that perform better are the ones of you singing in a higher register. Maybe the 20 percent of your work everyone seems to like are breakup songs.

Use this information however you see fit. I like to picture a Venn diagram. I'm constantly trying to find the overlap between what I feel compelled to do as a songwriter and artist, and what will give me the best chance of providing for my family.

— On Music City and the Industry —

THE PUB AND THE MASTER

The music industry is confusing. But if you understand these two concepts, you'll understand ninety percent of everything I've learned over the last ten years about making money from music.

The two things are the pub and the master.

In the biz, "pub" is shorthand for publishing; "Master" refers to the recording. Much of the money in music comes from these two things.

Publishing is intellectual property. It's the invention of the song; the lyrics and melody. The master is a sound recording of the intellectual property; a particular rendering.

Let's say a TV show wants to use a song you wrote. It pays $10,000 all in. "All in" means for both the pub and the master. Although you wrote it, you didn't record it. Somebody else did. So you own and control the pub, but not the master. You own half. If the TV show uses the song you'll be paid $5000.

Now let's say you recorded somebody else's song. You own the master, they own the pub.

A record label, TV show, ad agency, wedding videographer, etc. all need the rights holders of the pub and the master to sign off before they can use the song.

Ideally, you own as much of the pub and master as possible. Are you a kid writing songs in your bedroom, recording them on your laptop, and uploading them to the Internet? You own the publishing and the master. All the money is yours.

Did you cowrite a song with one other person, and that person is the artist whose recording is being used by a TV show for $10,000 "all in"? You get $2500; or half the pub.

Please bear in mind, I'm oversimplifying for the sake of clarity.

It can get incredibly confusing when you factor in songwriting and artist deals, percentages, and who owns exactly what. And we haven't even touched on how the market values for the pub and master vary depending on the media. For example, as I'm writing this, streaming on services like Spotify and Apple Music doesn't pay out equally per the pub and master. But these are the general principles for understanding the monetary value of a song.

— The Industry —

CURIOSITY AND CONSCIENCE

When it comes to your music career, you'll sometimes feel certain pressures: pressure to write about specific topics, pressure to use particular sounds in your recordings because they're "in," or to collaborate with someone because they'd be good for your "brand." So, keep in mind a metaphorical intersection.

The two "streets" are Curiosity and Conscience. If you're like me, you'll find that you do your best work at the corner of those two streets. Why? Curiosity gives you permission to chase the things that interest you. If they're interesting to you, they're likely interesting to someone else.

For example, lately I've been curious about the topic of assisted living. I keep having memories of my grandparents in the nursing home. As a songwriter, I'm trying to figure out what's universal in those memories. I don't know why I'm curious about this topic right now. All I know is that I think about it a lot. My bet is that there are others out there thinking about it too.

So what about the Conscience street? The Conscience street will help you avoid areas that might be off-limits. For me, it's when my proverbial "check engine" light comes on, and I start asking myself things like, "Am I just perpetuating gender stereotypes here?" or "Why am I using this synthesizer setting I despise?" Moreover, I might wonder why I've agreed to work with a writer whose work I don't particularly like. These internal debates usually relate to the music industry and monetization.

Nevertheless, the Conscience street shouldn't just be about avoiding restricted zones. It's also about helping you move toward places that don't always feel easy or logical, but areas you feel compelled to pursue. Take, for instance, the topic of assisted living.

I began writing a song about it. Will it be a hit? I can almost guarantee it will not. But it's at the corner of Curiosity and Conscience, and that's where I believe I do my best work.

Trust me, I'm not perfect. I've worked on projects I wish I hadn't. I've suppressed inspiration I was afraid to chase. You likely will too. But the point is to remember your own version of Curiosity and Conscience. My guess is that's where you do your best work and have the most valuable art to offer the world.

— On Music City and the Industry —

GO EASY ON THE VICTIM SONGS

I am a child of the nineties. I grew up listening to grunge and rock. As much as I love these genres, they contain a lot of "victim" songs. What are victim songs? Victim songs are those in which the singer complains a lot. They tend to be a bit cynical and judgmental and there isn't a whole lot of hope in the lyrics. As a teenager, you resonate with the lyrics because those songs tap into all the angst and emotion you feel. That's why a lot of us started writing songs!

So when I moved to Nashville, I had a lot of victim songs in my pocket. That was about it. I didn't know they were victim songs. I was just writing what I felt. I met with publishers and showed them my victim songs. I thought they'd love them.

They didn't love them.

They knew something I hadn't thought about: My songs only worked because I was singing them. It was art. Not songs for someone else to sing. The lyrics were too personal, too specific. At times, uncomfortably honest. Who wants to record someone else's diary? Nobody.

Since I was trying to sign a publishing deal and have a chance at others recording my songs, I had to learn to write "hero" songs. What are hero songs? Well, first off, they are songs in which the singer doesn't whine. The singer should be likable, relatable, doing things that inspire or encourage others. Think of the protagonist in your favorite movie. Sure, they may be in a struggle or have some problem, but they overcome it with dignity. They experience some kind of change in themselves and are better off for it. And we, the listeners, are better off for having vicariously gone through it with them.

If you want a publishing deal and the chance at others

recording your songs, focus on lyrics that put the singer in a positive light. Have them see the world with hope and optimism without being too cheesy. Even if they're going through struggles—losing a relationship or feeling overwhelmed by the state of the world—have them deal with it without blaming others or being vengeful. Have the chorus be something a crowd could chant or sing along to with a smile or their eyes closed.

Side note: I'm mainly talking about Top 40 Pop and Country radio. Obviously, not all hit songs are hopeful and positive. In fact, many Grammy-winning songs are not. For example, "Hello" by Adele, and "This Is America" by Childish Gambino. But these songs were written or at least cowritten by the artist. The lyrics are personal, reflective, and provocative. The vast majority of songs on Pop and Country radio—that are written or cowritten with someone *other than* the artist—are hero songs.

— On Music City and the Industry —

COULD MISTER ROGERS SING THIS?

I'm often asked to write songs for TV commercials. The thing about TV commercials is they're made by companies. And for the most part companies don't want to offend anyone or be controversial. They need lyrics with a positive message that speaks to as many walks of life as possible.

How do I write a song that's positive, inclusive, and as universal as possible? I ask myself, "Could Mister Rogers sing this?"

It's a useful question because it quickly filters out the vast majority of lyrics. Lyrics I may have been confused about suddenly clearly work or don't work. Let's face it, Mister Rogers probably wouldn't sing existential lyrics about whether we're all alone in the universe. He certainly wouldn't blame anybody or anything for his problems.

He would, on the other hand, sing about seeing the good in the world. He'd sing about being curious and full of wonder. He'd talk about friendship. He'd talk about facing adversity with honor.

I'm not saying you have to use the Mister Rogers filter for a song to be commercially viable. There are plenty of amazing and popular songs that Mister Rogers wouldn't sing. But if you want to write a song for the majority of TV commercials, then consider it. Also, it doesn't have to be Mister Rogers. That just works for me. Maybe yours is someone else. Oprah, Jesus, Ghandi, Dolly Parton. Anyone who embodies a spirit of kindness and inclusion.

— On Music City and the Industry —

THE "WILL I BE SUCCESSFUL" TEST

One day I was listening to a well-known business leader give a talk. He said that an indicator of whether a new business will succeed or fail has to do with what the owner obsesses over. Do they obsess over the potential profit and lifestyle, the freedom of being their own boss? Or do they obsess over the systems and processes that it will take to build the business? Do they geek out on the inner workings of solving a particular problem and helping people? If it's the latter, there's a much better chance of the business succeeding because their energy and excitement about the actual business will fuel it forward. The lifestyle perks will be a byproduct.

As a songwriter, do you envision the attention and adoration a song might bring you? Do you think about the lifestyles of the rich and famous and maybe songwriting is your ticket in? That likely won't be enough. On the other hand, if you're relentlessly curious about how to get a song onto paper, something tangible, and it excites you to think about the process, that's a great sign. If you wake up at 3 AM and write down a line you don't want to forget, that's a promising indicator of future success.

I don't say this to discourage you if you're someone who mostly thinks about people liking you for your songs. We all want to be liked. I just say that to set expectations. I would love to play guitar as well as Jimi Hendrix, but I'm not that interested in guitar playing. The adoration would feel good, but I don't have the discipline or love of guitar Hendrix had to put in the time and focus. He was obviously obsessed with the process and technique. All the glamor came as a byproduct of his obsession.

If you want to become a successful songwriter, obsess over songwriting, not adoration or becoming rich and famous.

— On Music City and the Industry —

CROSS YOUR FINGERS, BUT DON'T HOLD YOUR BREATH

There's always the potential for huge upswings in the music business. So, at the first sign of something exciting happening, the most useful phrase I can give you is, "Cross your fingers, but don't hold your breath."

Crossing your fingers is a way of acknowledging the small success of having somebody interested in your song. It could be a TV show inquiring about licensing it, or perhaps a major label artist is thinking of recording it for their next single.

On the other hand, holding your breath is the equivalent of putting too much energy and excitement into the moment. Keep in mind, nothing's happened yet. You need to keep working and producing new material. Imagine if your boss told you she's considering giving you a raise, and you said, "Fantastic! Do you mind if I take an early lunch to celebrate?"

Don't do that. Don't take an early lunch. Don't max out your credit cards. Nine times out of ten, the deal falls through. But those odds, over time, will start to add up.

So cross your fingers, but don't hold your breath.

— On Music City and the Industry —

SUSTAINING A CAREER

Just the other day, I had an opportunity to arrange a song for a commercial. As I thought about how the opportunity actually came to me, I had to go back fifteen years. It was a relationship made that long ago, which was yielding results now.

That's how long some opportunities take. The groundwork is laid over time. If you resort to hype and shiny objects, you'll have a hard time sustaining that over the long term.

Let's say you have an album coming out. How do you make a big splash? How do you cut through the noise and make sure it reaches its potential? Well, first off, make sure you've done your best on the art itself. Second, don't think so much about making a splash as much as a creating a rising tide, something that will build exponentially over time. Think long, not loud. The persistent whisper, consistent quality work, month after month, year after year. Not the ringing telephone. Not the kid doing a cannonball off the high dive.

Do this, and you'll be in business for a long time. Be inconsistent, flaky, only good some of the time, and your career will likely be a blip.

EPILOGUE

LESSONS FROM A HIT SONGWRITER'S FUNERAL

My songwriting mentor passed away in 2019. He was one of the most successful songwriters of the last decade, having written and produced hundreds of songs, many of which topped the Billboard charts.

On the flight home from his private memorial service, I realized something. Not one person I talked to mentioned any of his hit songs. Sure, they noted how great a songwriter he was, but there wasn't any mention of particular songs. The stories I heard were about how he treated people and how he made them feel loved.

It occurred to me that among your friends and family, nobody cares about your so-called trophies. They are proud of your achievements, of course, but they probably can't remember everything you've done and accomplished. They love you because of your relationship with them and who you are.

Some songwriters want to be remembered for their songs. I think I used to want that as well. But the longer I live, the more I realize that my greatest hits will be how I treated people and the relationships I was blessed to have.

APPENDIX: CHEAT SHEETS

"Never cut corners."

—My dad (an electrician; not a songwriter)

— Appendix: Cheat Sheets —

HOW TO GET UNSTUCK

Whenever I'm stuck on a song, I imagine my dad and me in the Beltrami Island State Forest in northern Minnesota. Growing up, that's where we'd go on the weekends to hunt partridge. My dad didn't own a pickup truck, but he used the family minivan as if it were one. We'd go down roads meant for ATVs.

Needless to say, we'd often get stuck.

The thing about being stuck in a rut is, you can't get unstuck by doing the same things, the normal things. You can't gun it. You spin your tires, and mud flies everywhere.

It's counterintuitive, but you go slow, barely touching the pedal. Then you go in reverse, then forward again until the weight of the car and the rocking motion gain traction and momentum. Pretty soon, you're making progress. And maybe that's enough to do the trick and get free.

But sometimes it just gets you a little less stuck. So you combine the rocking with dry sticks and logs. Sometimes I'd drive, and my dad would push. Sometimes we'd both push. Once in a while, we'd need help from others. My uncle Duane and his tow rope. Or a few extra people to push.

Getting unstuck in a literal rut is not unlike getting unstuck in a songwriting rut. You just have to figure out what things are equivalent to rocking or sticks, extra pushing—anything but spinning the tires.

This is a list of things I try whenever I'm stuck:

- Switch the key.
- Change the time signature (e.g., 4/4 to 6/8).
- Turn it into a fast song if it's slow and vice versa.
- Switch from guitar to piano or another instrument.

- Change the perspective of the singer. From "I" language to "you" or "we" language.
- Move the first verse to the second or move lines around like blocks.
- Invite a cowriter to join you.

If you're still stuck after you've tried all these, give it a rest. Come back to it later. Maybe by then the mud will have dried and hardened, and you can drive that minivan straight through!

— Appendix: Cheat Sheets —

INSTEAD OF THEORY LEARN THIS

Songwriting isn't about theory. Many professional songwriters don't even read music. I'm one of them. We often don't know the names of the chords we're playing on guitar or piano.

What many of us do know, however, are numbers. Numbers are based on the shape or position you're in rather than the key. They give you and easy way to communicate when collaborating.

What do I mean by "numbers"? I mean 1, 2, 3, 4, 5, 6, and 7. That's it. Think: do, re, mi, fa, so, la, ti (and do is back to 1). For a basic song, you only need 1, 4, 5, and 6.

Let's pretend you're in a cowriting session and your cowriter is playing in the key of G on guitar. Here's what the numbers would be:

G - 1
C - 4
D - 5
Em - 6

If you were in the key of D, it would look like this:

D - 1
G - 4
A - 5
Bm - 6

Why use numbers instead of the chord name? Well, you might be using C, F, and G shapes on the guitar. But you have a capo on, so you're actually in the key of Eb. Do you really want to transpose G to Eb to your piano player or electric guitarist? My brain hurts just thinking about it.

Memorize your numbers instead of actual theory. It saves time and mental energy and you'll avoid confusion.

Here's a quick guide:

KEY OF C

1 - C major: the root chord (this will be the key you're in)
2 - D minor: a less commonly used minor chord in progressions
3 - E minor: another less commonly used minor chord in progressions
4 - F major: commonly used in progressions
5 - G major: commonly used in progressions
6 - A minor: the most common minor chord used in progressions
7 - B major: a chord you'll rarely use; usually as a transition chord

A simple chord chart, then, would look like this:

Verse
1 - 4 - 1 - 4 (repeat 4x)

Chorus
1 - 4 - 6 - 5 (repeat 4x)

Bridge
6 - 5 - 6 - 5 (repeat 2x)

— Appendix: Cheat Sheets —

HOW TO STRUCTURE A BASIC SONG

If you're new to songwriting, just the thought of writing an entire song can be overwhelming. Where will you begin? How will you end? What will the middle look like?

Instead of thinking about the entire song, I like to break it down into shapes. For the most part, a song is made up of three basic shapes. Let's call them circles, squares, and triangles.

The circle is your first shape. Chord-wise, it's your verse progression and often your intro progression. Let's say the chord progression is G - C - D - G

So your song might start out like this:

INTRO   VERSE
○ ○   ○ ○ ○ ○

In other words, you'd play G - C - D - G twice in the intro and four times in the verse.

The next shape is your square. This is your chorus. More likely than not the chord progression will change. Let's say this progression is C - D - Em - G. After you'd played the intro and verse, you'd play:

CHORUS
☐ ☐ ☐ ☐

Each square represents playing through the progression once.

What happens after the chorus? It's called a "turnaround," which very commonly is just the intro played once, so:

TURNAROUND
○

After the turnaround, you're back into verse mode:

VERSE 2
○ ○ ○ ○

Then, yes…

CHORUS 2
☐ ☐ ☐ ☐

After the second chorus, a common song structure will have our third shape: the triangle.

What's the purpose of the triangle? To prevent your listener from getting bored. So far they've only heard circles and squares and if you keep it up they're going to lose interest. Our triangle, called a "bridge" or sometimes a "middle eight," is a chord progression that will usually start with something other than what the circle and square started with. So, to avoid that, let's say our triangle progression is Em - D - Em - D. It'd look like this:

BRIDGE
△ △ △ △

After you've played your triangle progression four times, your listener is ready to hear something familiar again, so bring back the square—only play it softly. Playing the chorus softly after the the bridge is called a "breakdown." It's to provide familiarity with tension and get your listener excited for the repeated chorus.

BREAKDOWN CHORUS
☐ ☐ ☐ ☐

Ok, you've played the breakdown chorus progression four times softly. Now, give the listener what they want. The chorus again, but loud!

REPEAT CHORUS
☐ ☐ ☐ ☐

At this point you're imagining everyone singing along and happy, but what happens when you finish singing this last chorus?

Go back to your intro, turnaround, and (now) outro chords for a bookend-type finish.

OUTRO
○○

That's it! Here's what the entire song would look like:

```
INTRO   VS     CH    TRNARND   VS2    CH2    BRDG    BRKDWN CH   RPT CH   OUTRO
○○    ○○○○  □□□□    ○○     ○○○○  □□□□   △△△△     □□□□     □□□□    ○○
```

Keep in mind, this is a common and basic song structure. Each genre tends to follow its own rules, and the rules are always changing. The singer/songwriter genre often has two or more verses before the first chorus (Tracy Chapman's "Fast Car"). Sometimes folk doesn't have a chorus, but more of a refrain at the end of each verse ("The Times They Are a Changin'" by Bob Dylan). In pop and country, the chorus often comes as quickly as possible. Some songs start with the chorus.

Side note: Before passing away, hit songwriter and teacher Ralph Murphy would would study all the number one records in pop and country for the current year to determine common threads. He'd generously share the information with songwriters, saying "survival of the craft of songwriting" was his primary goal.[1] Check out his book *Murphy's Laws of Songwriting* for more detailed information about the craft of writing hit songs for pop and country.

---

[1] Murphy, Ralph. "Structure in Number Ones." Nashville Songwriters Association International, https://www.nashvillesongwriters.com/structure-number-ones-0. Accessed 24 October 2023.

— Appendix: Cheat Sheets —

DO YOUR SONG THIS METADATA FAVOR

Your music is mostly digital files these days. You record on your iPhone, computer. Even if you record on a reel-to-reel tape machine, the music will eventually become a digital file. Rarely do we ever hold recorded music—a CD, vinyl record, tape, etc.— in our hands anymore. This is why metadata is important.

What's metadata? Metadata is the information within the digital file. If you were to open up an MP3 file in your media browser, it would look something like this screenshot:

Most songwriters and musicians don't care about these fields, aside from the song title and artist name. But it's important that you fill these fields out with as much information as possible. Why? As soon as you send a file, you're relinquishing control of that file: your song. The person you send it to—a friend, industry executive, music supervisor, whoever—might listen, then email or text it to someone else. This is a good thing because your song starts working on your behalf; it's an asset that develops relationships with people without you doing any more work. But then it will likely get lost, buried among all the other digital files deep within someone's inbox, hard drive, Dropbox, or wherever.

The reason the song title and artist name fields aren't sufficient is because the information is both too specific (the artist name) and too vague (the title). Those words won't surface when someone is doing an unrelated search within their database because the computer's search algorithm won't see your song as relevant. What you're trying to do by filling out your song's metadata is make the search algorithm bring it up along with other similar keyword files.

Here, let's give an example.

Say you wrote a song and sent it to a friend. They loved it, but then years pass. You both forgot about the song. It's buried somewhere on your friend's computer. But one day, this person is doing a search on their hard drive for a type of tomato seed they filed long ago, but can't remember the name. They type in "tomato" and, along with other tomato files, up comes your song called "The Garden." The reason your song also came up is because you'd entered all the lyrics in the metadata. The word tomato was used twice. Now, your friend, years later, sees your song again, listens and is reminded of how much they love it. They send it to another friend because it's the perfect song for the that season. What happens after that? Who knows.

Fill out your metadata. It's boring, I know. But if you do the work up front, you're giving your song a much better chance at having as many relationships with people as possible without you doing any more work. If you simply fill out the artist name and song title, you're risking the song being lost and forgotten.

Here's a quick checklist of things I recommend you include:

- The title of the song
- The artist performing the song

- Artwork (if the song has been officially released)
- The writer(s) of the song
- Performing rights affiliation
- Who owns the publishing (see "The Pub and the Master" on page 83)
- Who owns the master (see "The Pub and the Master" on page 83)
- Keywords (very important)
- Lyrics (mega important)

And here are a few screenshots of how I fill out my own metadata:

Help Me
Aaron Espe
Single

| Details | Artwork | Lyrics | Options | Sorting | File |

title: Help Me
artist: Aaron Espe
album: Single
album artist:
composer: 100% Aaron Espe (ASCAP IPI: 572361549)
☐ Show composer in all views
grouping: singer/songwriter, male vocals, acoustic guitar, fingerpicking, cello, strin
genre: Singer Songwriter
year: 2021
track: of
disc number: of
compilation: ☐ Album is a compilation of songs by various artists
rating: ☆☆☆☆☆ ♡
bpm: 120
play count: 0   Reset
comments: Publishing:
100% Crowd Goes Mild (ASCAP IPI: 381368935)
Master:
100% Aaron Espe

Cancel   OK

Help Me
Aaron Espe
Single

| Details | Artwork | Lyrics | Options | Sorting | File |

Album Artwork

HELP ME
AARON ESPE

< >   Add Artwork   Cancel   OK

Help Me
Aaron Espe
Single

| Details | Artwork | Lyrics | Options | Sorting | File |

Help me to love my neighbors
Help me love my enemies
Help me to bless those that curse me
Help me to turn the other cheek

Help me
Help me
Help me
Please
Help me

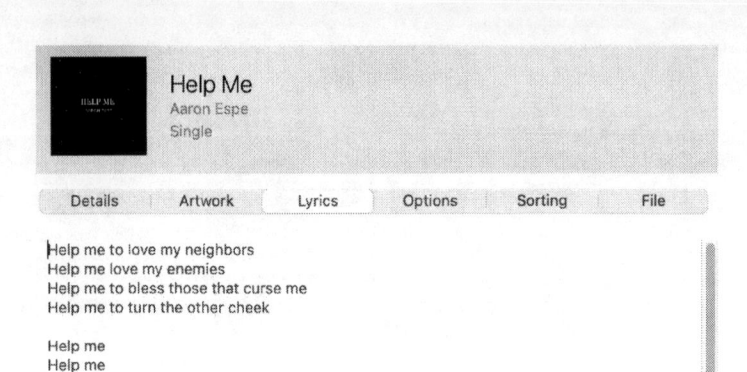

Help me to not be so angry
Help me to smile and laugh
Help me to choose something good
When I all I want is to choose something bad

Help me
Help me
Help me
Please
Help me

Help me have strength under pressure
When courage is put to the test
Help me when no one is watching
Help me even then do my best

Help me to speak less and listen
To honestly try understand
But then help me not to be silent
When my voice is all that I have

Help me

☑ Custom Lyrics   Cancel   OK

— Appendix: Cheat Sheets —

RULES FOR TV ADS

There are general rules to follow if you want your song to be used in a TV commercial. These rules aren't about making your song contrived; they're about steering it in a way that gives the song more options, future opportunities. Since I depend on music to feed my family, I'm keenly aware when writing a song whether that song could be commercially viable. If it does, I make sure to keep my options open and not paint the song into a corner. How? By following these rules:

1. Don't use proper nouns.
2. Keep the tempo above 90 beats per minute.
3. Don't use many specific, concrete images.
4. Think in general terms (up, down, here, there, etc.)
5. Stay positive but compelling, not cheesy.
6. Use your own real life, happy moments.
7. The less words the better.
8. Keep the language simple.
9. Could Mister Rogers sing it? If no, revise.
10. Don't write about romantic love.
11. Write about love for life.
12. Use "we" language when possible.
13. No whining.
14. No "I'm a victim" songs.
15. Friendship songs work.
16. A song secretly about your dog could work.

Bonus tip: I find it helpful to keep in mind the cheesy stock photograph of people that comes in a new picture frame. It's often of smiling happy people. That's NOT what you want to write. That will sound too plastic-like; too music-house and generic. Instead, replace that picture with a candid of your own family, smiling and enjoying life. Write the song version of that. Something real and personal. But also something in which people recognize themselves.

— Appendix: Cheat Sheets —

5 STRANGELY EFFECTIVE WRITING PROMPTS

These are prompts I've used when I wasn't feeling particularly inspired. Try a few out and see where they take you.

1. Go on YouTube and search "scenic drive." Choose a video of a passenger filming from their car window on a road trip. Something that feels like you're in the car with them. Put the volume on mute. Now start playing chords or humming little melodies, something that might sound like it'd be playing in the car. Write the type of song you'd want to listen to on this scenic drive.
2. Rewrite "This Land Is Your Land" with your own lyrics.
3. Go on Craigslist and search the "Community" section. Pick a title/listing that grabs your attention. For example, I just saw "Looking for someone to talk to." That could be a great song. "Someone to Talk To."
4. Open your phone's pictures app. Scroll back six months ago from today's date. Write the song version of that picture.
5. On the guitar, move your fingers up the neck without looking. Make random chord shapes until you stumble upon something that resonates with you. Write a song starting from this newly discovered chord.

ACKNOWLEDGEMENTS

Thank you to my wife, Heidi, for being my first reader and editor. And thank you to the following friends who read early drafts and offered valuable feedback and encouragement: Barry Dean, Doug Waterman, Isaac Slade, Ben West, Phillip Phillips, Leigh Nash, Bonnie Baker, Greta Morgan, Gregory Alan Isakov, Noah Kahan, Madi Diaz, Bre Kennedy, Brett Dennen, Fred Wilhelm, and Greg Gallo.

ABOUT THE AUTHOR

Aaron Espe is two Spanish courses short of his English degree. In 2004 he dropped out of the University of North Dakota to begin touring as a singer-songwriter. After burning out from the road and being diagnosed with a major anxiety and depressive disorder, he moved with his wife to Nashville, Tennessee, to try to make it as a working songwriter. He served coffee at Starbucks to stars like Taylor Swift and Keith Urban, and tuned pianos until eventually signing a publishing deal in 2012. His songs have been recorded by prominent artists across multiple genres, while his solo albums have amassed nearly one hundred million streams on Spotify and Apple Music, and have also been featured in numerous commercials and TV shows. He lives with his wife Heidi and their four sons in East Nashville, Tennessee.

To learn more, visit **aaronespe.com** or email him at a@aaronespe.com.

Made in United States
Troutdale, OR
01/17/2024